Cheers,
Annette M. Horrian

# THE ART OF TASTING WINE

WRITTEN AND ILLUSTRATED BY

ANNETTE DION MCGOWAN

First printing January 2012

ISBN-978-0-9836614-5-0

Published by

Vibrant Art Publishing

745 Trafton Road Moss Landing, CA 95039

831-239-0534 (phone)

831-724-5493 (fax)

VibrantArt@me.com

Dedicated to

my family and friends,

who encourage me to pursue

my dreams!

# Introduction

I have been wine tasting most of my life. My father made wine at home from fruit grown in our orchard. I can remember plastic tubes running from one bottle to the next in the small green house where the wine was brewed. When my parents were out of sight I would sneak into the green house and suck on the tubes. I liked the apricot and plum wine the best. I was less than five years old at the time and had no idea what wine was. However, even at a young age I knew which wines I liked. Being intrigued by wine and a connoisseur at such a young age may explain a lot.

In my twenties I enjoyed having blind wine tasting parties. I would have each guest bring a bottle of wine disguised in a paper bag. The bags were then numbered and everyone would rate the wines and write comments about each. There would be a prize for the best red wine and one for the best white wine. There was also a booby prize for the worst wine. The booby prize was usually awarded to my brother, Jack, for bringing a bottle of Thunderbird.

The comments at those parties were unsophisticated, yet truthful. As the night grew long and fuzzy, the comments became more honest and less legible. "This tastes like it was filtered through dirty underwear" (I am sure it must have been the Thunderbird) or "this wine is yum yum yummy." In my twenties I didn't know there was an art to or a ritual for tasting wine. A proper way to See, Swirl, Sniff, Sip, Swish and yes, Spit wine.

Oh, so sophisticated. I had no clue there was a special language used while tasting wine called "Wine Speak." If I had only known, I am sure I would have chosen "Wine Speak" for my foreign language in school.

I am writing this book to provide you with an enjoyable, yet effective way to learn the language and art of tasting wine. There is an incredible amount of information available on wine and wine tasting (see Appendix A for recommended reading). This book will be covering the basics. Nonetheless, by reading this book and practicing what it recommends you can become proficient in the basics of tasting wine. I hope to provide you with enough knowledge and new vocabulary that you will be able to taste and describe wine with confidence, using "wine speak." Heaven forbid you ever embarrass yourself at a wine tasting by saying something so simple and honest as, "this wine stinks." Or have people wonder why you know what something tastes like that was filtered through dirty underwear. After reading this book you will know to say "this wine has a dirty nose" or "I detect a bouquet of a barnyard" to express the same sentiment correctly, and thus impress even the most sophisticated company with your savoir faire.

I hope that I assist you in finding a new appreciation for the nectar of the grape. May this book (along with a little wine) put a smile on your face as you discover,

*The Art of Tasting Wine*

Cheers, *Annette*

# Table of Contents

# How to get the most out of this book

This book is designed to provide you with a fun, hands on approach for learning to taste wine. To enhance your enjoyment you may want to have some friends join you while tasting.

The following is a list of supplies you will need to have available while tasting wine.

- A few bottles of different wines
- A cork screw
- Some clean, clear wine glasses
- A small notebook
- A vase with a wide mouth opening or a small bucket
- Some tissue or a handkerchief
- Water, plain crackers or bread to clear your palate between tasting different wine.
- Optional: chocolate, cheese and fruit to eat while tasting wine.

# Gather your supplies & pop a cork, class is in session

Start by taking notes while you evaluate the first wine you taste. Write down the wine maker, the type or name of the wine, the vintage (year the wine was created) and the wine's place of origin. This information can be found on the label. You may also want to include the price. See Appendix C in the back of this book for an example of a Wine Tasting form.

Use a page of notes for each wine. Write about each of the "Ss" or steps used to become familiar with a wine. Most importantly, note whether you like the wine and why. After you have tasted several wines review your notes, looking for patterns. Soon you will see what types of wine you prefer, and understand why.

# Sex or making love, which do you prefer?

Tasting a glass of wine is similar to drinking a glass of wine in many ways. However, it is significantly different. There is a mindfulness to tasting wine which is often overlooked while merely drinking wine. When tasting wine you open yourself up to the romance and subtle nuances found in the wine. These subtleties often go unnoticed when drinking wine. When tasting wine you are reading the poetry of the grape as you unveil the art of the wine maker. Drinking wine is like having sex, while tasting wine is like making love. One "hits the spot" and the other is something you savor.

For a long time I missed out on fully enjoying many of the wonderful qualities of different wines. I was not paying enough attention to notice them. I was oblivious to the fact that to appreciate wine fully, and unravel the mysteries of a wine, I needed to be aware of what I was doing while tasting. Fortunately, I saw the light and now follow a system, or ritual for tasting wine. This system has dramatically enhanced my ability to enjoy wine.

The system begins with relaxing and opening up to a satisfying encounter with wine. I then look at, smell and taste the wine, creating a memorable connection. Nothing too complicated. However, there is a specific way to perform each step to achieve the most satisfying results.

*Pay attention and don't forget to take notes.*

# Learning to taste wine is as simple as
## *S S S S S*

Wine tasting uses most of your senses, not just your taste buds. Smell and sight play a big part in the tasting experience. Touch tells you about the "mouth feel" and the temperature of the wine. When tasting champagne you can use your sense of hearing to listen to the music of bubbles popping.

Whether enjoying an expensive bottle of wine at a fine restaurant or visiting a tasting room, the ritual for tasting wine is the same. Just remember *S S S S S S* or the six "*S*s." To help you remember the six "*S*s," I would like you to say the following words in the following sequence. You get extra points if you say them with a lisp and you turn your nose up slightly in the air.

*See-Swirl-Sniff, Sip-Swish-Spit (or Swallow)*

Now say them again five times real fast. After you have been wine tasting for a while, try saying them again five times real fast without spitting on anyone.

# TILTED

# The first S is for SEE

## A revealing look

"See" refers to looking at the color and clarity of the wine. Just one look can tell you a lot about a wine. It can reveal some things about how the wine was processed. A wine's color comes from the skin of the grape. The skin of grapes are left on while making red wines and removed when making white. A look can also give you hints about the age of a wine. As red wines age they becomes lighter. As white wines age they grow darker. Pour an ounce or two of wine into a clean clear wine glass. Hold your wine glass by the stem to avoid warming the wine with your hand. Being careful not to spill your wine, tilt your glass slightly to one side and look at the color and clarity of the wine. This works best if the background behind the wine glass is a light color. For clarity you are looking at the opacity and checking for any visibly suspended particles. A clear very young white wine may be as colorless as water. A red wine that has passed its peak of maturity may have a brown color at the outer edge or rim of the wine glass.

*We show our age when we wear rimmed glasses.*

*Wine shows its age at a glass's rim.*

# Wine Speak descriptors for the color and clarity of wine

**Bright:** When describing the visual appearance of wine, bright refers to clarity with very low levels of suspended particles. Drinking a bright wine will not make you any brighter. Reading this book might.

**Brilliant:** A brilliant wine is completely clear and transparent. Brilliance is not always a positive characteristic. The absence of any suspended particles may also indicate an absence of flavor. Drinking brilliant wine will not make you brilliant. However, reading this book may help.

**Browning:** In wine, browning is a sign of age. If you see a hint of brown, at the surface edge of a tilted wine glass, it indicates that the wine has passed its peak. You can still drink the wine, however some of its flavor and freshness may have faded.

**Clear:** Describes a wine with no visible particles. Drinking clear wine can make your thinking less clear.

**Cloudy:** Cloudy is the opposite of clear. In a wine it is considered a fault. Cloudy wine may signal a problem such as bacteria. Drinking cloudy wine will make your thinking cloudy.

**Crust:** Crust is sediment that adheres to the inside of a wine bottle. A crusty wine is usually drinkable. However you may want someone else to take the first sip.

**Hazy:** Hazy wine is full of suspended particles. Some wines are unfiltered and are therefore expected to be hazy. Drinking hazy wine can make your thoughts hazy.

**Inky:** Inky wine has a dark color, and is often opaque. If it spoils, use it as watercolor paint. I discovered this use of inky wine one day when I was enjoying a glass while I was painting. After accidentally dipping my brush in my wine I was pleasantly surprised by the rich color my brush left on the paper. If I had accidentally sipped the water used to clean my paint brush, I am sure my surprise wouldn't have been as pleasant.

**Rim:** Rim refers to the color at the edge of the wine in a glass. The rim helps in determining the age of a wine.

CLOUDY

# The second $S$ is for SWIRL
## and the search for tears

Gently Swirl the wine around. Make sure that it coats the upper part of your glass. Hold your glass at eye level for 3-5 seconds while you look for legs or tears. Tears or legs are the colorless streams of liquid that cling to the sides of a glass after the contents have been swirled. They are related to the content of the alcohol in a wine and have nothing to do with a wine's quality. The thicker the tears the higher the alcohol content of the wine.

WINE WITH NICE LEGS

ANNETTE DION

# The third $S$ is for SNIFF
## Pleasant or putrid, it's all in the nose of the beholder

Set your glass on a hard surface such as a table or counter. Again, swirl the wine this time with your hand over the top of the glass. While the wine is still moving, remove your hand and put your nose close to the glass (slightly inside is acceptable). Quickly inhale two or three times and smell the vapors of the wine. This is the Sniff. (For an alternate sniffing technique see Wine Tasting Adventures, Avila Beach, California, Day One.) Does the wine have a smell? If you can't smell much you would say the wine is closed, dumb, holding back or reticent. There is always the possibility you are coming down with a cold and your nose is stuffed up. Closed, dumb or reticent wines are usually young. A young wine's subtle scent is referred to as its aroma. Mature wines are more fragrant. When describing the smell of a mature wine you refer to their bouquet.

Does the wine smell good to you? There are no right or wrong answers here. Whether you like the smell or taste of a wine is entirely subjective. If you preferred chocolate cake for dessert over cheese cake no one would say you are wrong. The same goes for wine. Only your nose knows what smells you prefer.

If the wine smells good to you, say that it has a nice bouquet or a good nose. A wine's nose is its overall aroma or bouquet. You may even say the wine is clean. Clean wine does not contain undesirable smells.

Aromas you will discover in a wine include: fruits, herbs, spices, flowers, earth, grass, tobacco, smoke, candy, vanilla, coffee and chocolate. You may also find negative aromas such as diesel fuel, vinegar, rotten eggs or a dirty barn.

WINE WITH A NICE BOUQUET

WINE WITH A GOOD NOSE

COLOSSEUM
Chianti

CESAR'S DEN
Rome ITALY

If you don't like the smell of the wine don't say it stinks. Such language is unacceptable. "Stinks" is not a term included in the language of Wine Speak. You may say that a wine smells acidic, corked, or like rotten eggs. You might get away with saying the wine has the essence of putrescence. Or, you can say that wine "smells like a barnyard." But don't say that wine stinks unless you want everyone to know you are a rookie. Learning Wine Speak isn't always easy. Don't kill the teacher. I didn't make up the rules. Who made the rules, anyway?

Acidic is a vinegary smell. Wine turns to vinegar when over exposed to air. Corked means it has a rotten or disgusting aroma. "Rotten eggs" means the wine smells like, well, rotten eggs. The term barnyard refers to a certain unmistakable odor of an unclean stable, pig sty or chicken coop. You know the smell if you have ever driven by a dairy or walked into a bathroom just after uncle Ted has left. No, you can't say the wine smells like _____ either. However, you can say it has the bouquet of a barnyard. Isn't Wine Speak lovely?

*Are you remembering to take notes?*

BARNYARD WINE

20

Now that you have decided whether or not you like the bouquet of the wine, let's have some fun and take this a step further and describe what you smell. A wine's taste is influenced as much by the fruit it is made from as from the wine making process.

When you are at a tasting room and there is a description of the wine on the flight menu (a list of wines you will be tasting) don't read it. It is much more fun if you smell and taste the wine and write your own assessment down, before you look at the description. See if your description matches the menu.

Sometimes I think the person writing the descriptions has taste buds numbed from too much alcohol. Other times, everything matches perfectly.

*Don't forget to take notes.*

# Wine Speak descriptors that refer to the aroma or bouquet of wine

You may notice that many of the descriptors for smell also refer to taste.

**Apple:** The aroma and taste of fresh apples is commonly found in Chardonnays and Rieslings.

**Baked:** A wine is called baked when it smells or tastes like cooked fruit, similar to some Sherrys. This is often the result of hot climates, where the grapes are either overripe or have sat out in the hot sun after harvesting. In some wines a baked taste may be good, in others it is considered a fault.

**Biscuity:** Some mature Champagnes have a bouquet with a hint of yeast or smell like fresh bread dough or biscuits. This is considered a good trait.

BAKED

23

DIFFUSE

**Blowzy:** An overpowering fruity aroma, associated with low quality fruity wines. I remember in my teens drinking a wine called Boons Farm, Strawberry Hill. This would definitely fall into the category of blowzy. I haven't seen that wine in decades. Perhaps, it's not made anymore or, at this point in my life, I migrate to the section of higher quality wines in stores.

**Cheesy:** An aroma of mild or nutty cheese often found in aged champagnes.

**Chocolaty:** A term most often used with rich red wines. This descriptor describes the aromas, flavors and silkiness of chocolate.

**Citrusy:** A wine with aromas and flavors of citrus fruits.

**Cedar:** Fine red wines often have a bouquet of cedar wood.

**Cloves:** An aroma of cloves can be found in wines aged in toasted oak barrels.

**Diesel:** If the wine smells or tastes like the fumes from the exhaust of an old school bus this is the descriptor you would use. It is most common in Riesling wines. In small amounts some people consider this to be a positive characteristic. They are the same people, who as kids, stood behind school busses inhaling the fumes hoping to get a buzz. As adults they drink wine hoping for the same thing.

**Diffuse:** A diffuse wine is a wine with smells and tastes that lack focus and structure. This is often because a wine is being served too warm. Wine is usually best served between 50 and 60 degrees Fahrenheit. It is okay to serve red wine slightly chilled. If it is hot out ask your waiter for an ice bucket to keep your wine chilled.

EARTHY

CELESTIAL BLEND

6000BC

DEVINE CREATIONS

GARDEN OF EDEN

**Dirty:** A wine with unpleasant flavors and aromas that resulted from poor hygiene during the wine making process.

**Earthy:** An earthy wine has aromas and flavors of the earth such as those found in a forest floor or a freshly plowed field.

# GRAPEY

**Foxy:** A negative term used to describe a wine with a musty, moth ball odor or flavor.

**Fruity:** A wine whose aromas and flavors suggest fruit. Do not confuse with blowsy which is an overpowering bouquet or taste of fruit.

**Grapey:** A wine with the aromas and flavors of grape jelly. Imagine that, some wines made from grapes taste like grapes.

**Grassy:** A term used to describe wine that has the aroma or flavor of freshly cut grass.

**Herbaceous:** A wine that has the aromas and flavors of herbs and vegetation. This is a "wine speak" word I love to say. If you master this one they may even let you into Frazer and his brother Niles' wine club.

**PEPPERY**

**Licorice:** A term used to describe the aroma and flavor of licorice or anise. Most often found in sweet wines.

**Linalool:** A flowery peach aroma associated with Muscat and Riesling wines. It is derived from the chemical compound linalool which is naturally found in flowers. This is one of the descriptors I most enjoy saying when tasting wine. It just rolls off my tongue (if I have not been tasting very long) sounding like I know something about wine. Linalool, Linalool, Lin-A-Loooool.

**Moldy:** If a wine smells moldy don't drink it!

**Oxidized:** An oxidized wine describes a wine that has been overexposed to air and is no longer fresh. It is considered faulty and may have sherry like odors or may have turned to vinegar.

**Peppery:** A wine that smells or tastes like peppers or freshly ground pepper.

**Perfumey:** A positive term used to describe a wine with a pleasant floral aroma or bouquet.

**Sherry like:** A term used to describe a non Sherry wine that smells like Sherry, resulting from being overexposed to air.

PERFUMEY

*31*

**Smoky:** is a term used to describe aromas and flavors of different types of smoke, such as tobacco or smoke from a campfire. Smoky aromas and flavors are found in oak treated wines.

**Soy sauce:** A wine with the aroma of soy sauce.

**Spicy:** Unlike spicy food which has a hot flavor, a spicy wine has aromas and flavors of spices such as cinnamon and cloves. This can come from the type of grapes used to make the wine or from aging the wine in oak.

**Tar:** A wine with aromas and flavors of tar.

**Vanilla:** A wine with aromas and flavors of vanilla.

**Vegetal:** A wine with aromas and flavor of vegetation.

Blue Ridge
Estate

BOUDOIR
BORDEAUX

S
M
O
K
Y

33

**WOODSY**

Woodsy: A wine with aromas found in the woods.

Yeasty: A wine with aromas and flavors of bread dough or biscuits.

Zesty: A zesty wine is lively with aromas of citrus fruit.

# Sip and Swish
## the forth S is for Sip and
## the fifth S is for the Swish

After you have taken a good look at the wine and sniffed it properly, it is time to Sip. I said sip, not guzzle. Take a sip of the wine. Swish it around your mouth to clear your palette. Then take a second sip. Hold it in your mouth. What is the first taste you experience? Is it different from the wine's bouquet? How does it feel in your mouth? Is it coarse, thick and syrupy or thin and light? Does it make your mouth pucker or your tongue feel fuzzy?

The weight or mouth feel of the wine is called the body. The body is often attributed to the wine's alcohol content. You can classify a wine as light bodied, medium bodied or full bodied. A light bodied wine contains low levels of alcohol and sugars. If a wine is watery or thin with little flavor you would describe it as having a light body. A full bodied wine lets you know that it is there. It is rich in alcohol and sugar and has a bold taste. A medium bodied wine falls somewhere in between.

SUCKER

Now swish your wine around and treat all your taste buds to the wine's flavors. Does anything change? Are different tastes coming through? At this point I prefer to aerate my wine with a gargle. This has caused me to receive looks of disgust from die hard wine weenies. Unfortunately, even some of my friends take this as a cue to cut me off from tasting more wine. If you choose to gargle consider your surroundings. In restaurants I recommend aerating wine by sucking air through your teeth, in a modified, almost silent gargle. Practice at home first, so that if you accidentally aspirate some wine and find yourself uncontrollably coughing, you won't stain your fancy, out in public clothes.

Okay then, let's practice. Here we go. While keeping the wine in your mouth, gently breathe out through your nose. Keep your teeth together, part your lips, and quickly suck some air in through your teeth. Don't worry if your first try is, well, messy. That's why you're practicing at home. Just try it again. With a little more practice you will find that you have become a first class sucker. Aerating wine usually brings out flavors one simply can't experience any other way. That's why this step is necessary to fully enjoy and appreciate fine wine.

*Write some more notes in your notebook.*

# Wine Speak descriptors that refer to taste

**Acidic:** A wine that is tart or sour with a noticeable amount of acidity.

**Bitter:** An unpleasant taste of tannins. Imagine chewing on grape seeds. That is what tannins taste like.

**Buttery:** A wine that has a rich, creamy mouth feel with flavors similar to butter.

**Concentrated:** An intensely flavorful wine.

**Coarse:** A term for a wine with a strong taste of tannins and a rough mouth feel.

**Flinty:** A wine with a metallic taste.

**Honeyed:** A wine which tastes like honey.

**Lemony:** A wine which is tart and tastes of lemons.

**Minerality:** A wine with flavors reminiscent of mineral water. Wines with mineral undertones are better to drink with food than to drink naked. The food softens the mineral taste in the wine and the mineral taste in the wine enhances the food. I know what you're thinking. What in the world does drinking wine naked have to do with drinking wine with food? Can't you do both at the same time? Don't worry I haven't completely lost my mind. Drinking wine "naked" is a wine speak term for drinking wine without any food to accompany it. So before you disrobe at the speed of light when some cute thing asks you if you want to drink some wine naked, make sure of what they want naked. You, the wine or both.

40

# DRINKING WINE NAKED

**Oaky:** A wine that has a smoky oak flavors: This comes from treatment with oak.

**Steely:** A wine that has picked up a metallic taste from processing in steel containers.

**Tannic:** A red wine that is full and leaves your mouth feeling dry and coarse.

**Tart:** a perception of acid or sourness in wine.

**Tropical:** A wine that possesses flavors of tropical fruits.

41

# The sixth *S* is for SPIT
## to spit or not to spit, that is the question

Now that you have bonded with your wine you must choose whether to Spit or Swallow it. When tasting wine it is unnecessary to swallow because you have no taste buds in your throat or stomach. It is a good idea to spit if you are the designated driver or if you experience ill effects from drinking wine. Otherwise I vote for the swallow. I seem to have more fun when I swallow. However, I have had many wonderful times tasting wine with friends when I have been the designated spitter.

Tasting rooms usually have metal or ceramic spittoons. They look like large vases or buckets, on the counters of their wine bars. This is where it is appropriate to spit or to pour out the wine, from your tasting glass, that you don't want to drink. A word of caution. Some tasting rooms have tip jars on the counter which can be easily confused with a spittoon.

If you are averse to spitting in public you might want to practice at home first. See if you can master a dainty spit, or a manly spit. If you are single and hoping to meet someone special (real special) while tasting wine, you may want to practice a sexy spit. If you are reading this book with friends, this is the perfect opportunity to evaluate each others spitting technique. When spitting I advise against making loud hacking noises, unless you are trying to get the attention of that cute guy or girl across the wine tasting bar. When you are sure that they have noticed you, do your best sexy come hither spit, that you practiced at home, and invite me to the wedding.

Another tip on spitting is to drink a lot of water between your wine tasting so your saliva stays thin. There is nothing worse than being at a fancy wine tasting, getting the attention of the cute guy or girl across the room, with some artful hacking, then having them watch you do your sexiest spit, only to end up with a string of saliva connecting your mouth to the spittoon. You can see why I vote for the swallow. Fear not. A quick fix for this situation is to always carry a quick release tissue or handkerchief when wine tasting.

If you find even after practicing that you have no talent for spitting, you can skip spitting all together. Swallow the first sip. If the wine is absolutely awful go ahead and make a sour face and quiver a bit as you swallow while you pour the remaining wine out of your tasting glass and into the bucket. After you have spit or swallowed, evaluate the impression left in the back of your throat. This is called the finish or aftertaste. A good wine leaves a taste which lingers in your mouth to savor.

I know I am writing this book and should be the expert but can someone please explain to me why you can spit when tasting wine but you can't gargle. Personally I think we need to change a few things about wine tasting. The first thing I suggest is to add gargling. Not loud forceful gargling which spews wine from the taster's mouth, but gentle gargling to enhance the taste of the wine. If you agree with me, gargle away and maybe we can alter the ritual of tasting wine. It's worth a try.

*Remember to take more notes.*

# Some more things you should know about tasting wine

Whether you like or do not like a wine may be because of the balance or structure of the wine. You may prefer a sweet balance to your wine rather than a tart balance. The balance is a state of equilibrium or harmony between the main components in a wine—tannins, acid, sweetness and alcohol. When a wine is balanced one component does not overpower the others.

Similar to balance is structure. The structure of the wine relates to the equilibrium of the body and mouth feel of wine. Once again your preference of structure of a wine is subjective. You want to feel that there is something of substance in your mouth. A wine that is silky smooth and soft may not have enough structure for some. Others may find this heavenly. Tannins provide structure and some coarseness to the mouth feel of the wine.

WELL BALANCED

45

# Other words used to describe wine

**Accessible:** A wine that is smooth, balanced and easy to drink without an overwhelming taste of tannins, acid or alcohol.

**Aggressive:** A wine that is harsh with strong flavors and tannins. It is the opposite of a wine that is soft.

**Astringent:** An excessively tannic or dry white wine.

**Austere:** An unbalanced wine with excessively harsh acids or tannins.

**Big:** A wine with intense flavors and high in alcohol content. Similar to full bodied.

**Bite:** An interpretation of tannins or acidity in a wine. This can be either positive or negative depending on the wine's overall balance and taster's preference.

**Charming:** A subjective term used to describe a wine that is pleasing.

**Chewy:** A wine with tannins which are not overwhelming.

**Concoction:** A negative term used for an unbalanced wine with many different components.

**Connected:** A wine that discloses its region of origin.

**Compact:** A wine with a dense perception of fruit that is balanced by the weight of the other components in the wine.

**Complete:** A balanced wine with a pleasing weight and a long finish.

C
O
M
P
L
E
X

48

**Complex:** A Complex wine contains many intriguing subtle aromas and flavors which are usually well balanced and pleasing. It is a type of wine that you enjoy drinking, and, like a good mystery novel, you find it hard to put down.

**Classic:** A high quality wine that displays the characteristics of its varietals and is balanced and complex.

**Cloying:** A negative term, which describes a wine which is sickly sweet.

**Creamy:** A term used to describe a wine with a smooth, rich mouth feel.

**Crisp:** A wine term often associated with white wines and describes a refreshing acidity.

**Delicate:** A term used to describe a light, pleasing wine with subtle undertones.

**Direct:** A direct wine is one that reveals all its characteristics with your first smell and taste.

**Dried up:** A wine that is no longer fresh and has lost some flavor due to extended aging.

**Dry:** A dry wine is the opposite of sweet. It may have strong tannins or acid.

**Easy:** A direct, non complex wine that is pleasing and enjoyable to drink.

**Edgy:** A wine with an acidic balance that enhances the flavors of the wine.

**Elegant:** A wine that has many subtle flavors which are balanced.

**Elusive:** A wine with aromas and flavors which are difficult to identify.

**Expansive:** A wine with full flavors that remains easy to drink.

**Expressive:** A wine with aromas and flavors which are easy to identify.

E L U S I V E

**Faded:** A faded wine is past its peak and has lost some of its bouquet and flavor.

**Fallen over:** A young wine that has already passed its peak.

**Fat:** A full bodied wine with a thick mouth feel.

**Flabby:** A fat wine that is not balanced by acidity.

# FLAT

**Flat:** A sparkling wine that has lost its effervescence, or a wine that is lacking flavor and acidity.

*Green:* A green wine is young and has not aged long. A green wine is often light bodied and closed.

*Hard:* A wine with an over abundance of tannins.

*Harsh:* A derogatory term used to describe a wine that is unbalanced and overly tannic or acidic.

*Heavy:* A wine full in body and excessively alcoholic.

*Hollow:* A wine that lacks fruit undertones or flavor.

*Hot:* A wine with a sense of too much alcohol.

H
O
T

LIGHT

56

**Jammy:** A wine which is rich in fruit and low in tannins.

**Juicy:** A sweet balanced wine rich in fruit flavors and light in alcohol.

**Laid Back:** A California wine that is balanced and easy to drink.

**Lean:** A light wine with an acidic balance.

**Light:** A wine that has little alcohol or flavor.

**Lively:** A term used to describe a young wine that is tart and slightly carbonated.

**Luscious:** A full bodied wine with a sweet balance and a rich thick mouth feel.

**Mature:** A wine that has been aged to its peak point of quality.

**Mean:** A wine that is high in acid or tannins, out of balance and unpleasant to drink.

**Mellow:** A smooth wine that is pleasant to drink and near its peak of maturity.

**Nervy:** A tart wine that is balanced with the rest of the wine's components.

**Oily:** A wine with a viscous mouth feel.

RACY

**Opulent:** A rich, flavorful wine that has a pleasing texture and is well balanced.

**Palate:** A tasting term which refers to the mouth feel and taste of a wine.

**Peak:** The point in age where a wine is most ideal to drink.

**Polished:** A well balanced wine with a smooth mouth feel.

**Powerful:** A wine with a high alcohol content, which does not taste excessively alcoholic. Watch out for powerful wines as they tend to sneak up on you.

**Prickly:** A young wine with a slight effervescence, yet not enough to be considered a sparkling wine.

**Racy:** A tart wine that is well balanced with other components.

**Rich:** A slightly sweet, balanced wine.

**Robust:** A term with similar connotations as aggressive except robust is more commonly applied to older, mature wines, while aggressive tends to describe younger wines.

**Round:** A wine that is full bodied and smooth.

**Sassy:** A wine with bold "in your face" flavors.

**Sharp:** A term normally used to describe a wine with a high degree of tartness or bitterness.

**Short:** A full bodied wine with a lack of after taste.

**Soft:** A wine with low acid content that has a smooth mouth feel.

**Stalky:** A wine with woodsy or herbaceous undertones.

**Strong:** A wine that is full of flavor and rich in alcohol.

**Supple:** A wine that has a mild amount of tannins.

**Tannic:** A wine with a strong presence of tannins.

**Thin:** A wine with a watery mouth feel and little flavor.

**Tight:** A wine with a strong presence of tannins that hides the other qualities in the wine. Tight young wines often soften with age.

**Typicity:** A wine that has the typical characteristics of the varietal of grapes used in creating the wine.

**Undertone:** An undertone is a subtle flavor mixed in with more dominant flavors. A great wine may have many undertones.

**Up front:** A wine with characteristics which are easy to discover.

**Voluptuous:** A wine with a full body, rich mouth feel and a long finish.

**Warm:** A balanced wine with a noticeable amount of alcohol.

**Watery:** A wine that has a thin body and lacks flavor.

**Zippy:** A wine with a noticeable amount of tartness which is balanced with enough fruit to be pleasing.

# SMELLY AIR

# Choosing a wine
## So many wines, so little time

If you find picking out a wine a daunting task, you may want to consult with a Sommelier. A Sommelier pronounced "So-mal-yeah," or "smelly air" (when they are out of hearing distance) is a professional wine expert; which can be of great help when it comes to choosing a wine. You will find Sommeliers working in fine restaurants and wine stores. You only need tell them what type of wine you like, such as a complex full bodied red with a hint of cherries and a silky finish for a specified price point and the Sommelier should be able to recommend something you will like.

If you have a friend that is a passionate wine connoisseur (lay person knowledgeable about wine with discriminating taste) you may want to ask for their assistance when picking out a wine. It will make them feel important and you will end up with a good bottle of wine.

I would not recommend consulting with a wine con-o-sewer (a wine-o) when choosing a bottle of wine or you are likely to end up with a bottle of Thunderbird.

One trick I have used over the years is to choose a reserve. When a winery thinks one of their wines is pretty special they call it a reserve. If the experts think their wine is special it usually is. To help guide those who won't ask for directions or advice, I have outlined on the following pages what to expect from different wines.

# BOTTLES

# What to expect from popular WHITE wines

**Chardonnay:** (shar-doe-nay) A full body, dry white wine often buttery with undertones of fruit and oak.

**Chenin Blanc:** (sheh-nan blahnk) A crisp, fresh wine that has light notes of fruit and nuts. The mouth feel is slightly oily.

**Gewurtztraminer:** (ga-VERTZ-trah-mee-ner) A ligh to medium bodied, slightly sweet wine with an exotic symphony of flavors. You will find complex undertones of various fruits and spices.

**Moscato:** (muss-cot-toe) A sweet desert wine with an oily mouth feel and a long finish. Flavors are often rich with fruit with floral undertones.

**Muscat:** (moos-cat) A sweet medium bodied wine with a viscous mouth feel and fragrant bouquet. Undertones may include flowers, fruits and spices.

**Pinot Grigio**: (pee-no gree-joe) A light bodied, dry, crisp white wine with a flowery fragrance. The acidic balance gives the wine's fruit undertones a pleasant character. This wine is made to drink at a young age.

**Riesling:** (rees-ling) A light, refreshing white wine with fruit and floral undertones. Rieslings are wines that may include flavors of petrol or diesel which can be pleasant and enhance the wines' overall palate.

**Sauvignon Blanc:** (saw-vee-nyonh blahnk) A medium bodied, dry white wine with grassy, herbaceous flavors and undertones of tropical fruit and minerals.

**Viognier:** (vee-ohn-YAY) Known for its sweet floral perfume like aroma. This wine is often drier than its nose would suggest.

# What to expect from popular RED wines

**Beaujolais:** (bow-zhuh-LAY) A light, young, fruity wine which is low in alcohol. It is not intended for aging; it is meant to be consumed at a young age.

**Cabernet Sauvignon:** (cah-burr-NAY sow-vee-NYOHN) A flavorful, full bodied, complex dry wine, with flavors of plums, cherries and berries. Cabernets may have woodsy, earthy, chocolatety, peppery or smoky undertones.

**Cabernet Franc:** (cah-burr-NAY FRAHN) A medium to full bodied red wine with complex flavors which may include pepper, tobacco, raspberries and violets. You may find the mouth feel of this wine to be coarse.

**Malbec:** (MALL-beck) A medium to full bodied wine with a tapestry of rich, smooth, spicy flavors and undertones of berries, cherries, chocolate, plum and tobacco.

**Merlot:** (mer-LOW) A medium to full bodied wine with rich flavors of blackberries, cherries, plums and chocolate. You may also find spicy, floral and earthy undertones.

**Pinot Noir:** (pee-no NWAHR) A flavorful medium bodied wine usually aged in oak. Often complex, Pinot Noirs' flavors may include berries, cherries, chocolate, smoke, pepper, vanilla and numerous other undertones.

**Sangiovese:** (san-joe-VAY-zee) A light to medium bodied red wine that is usually lighter in color than many other red wines. It has a light fruit flavor because the grapes are acidic. You may find undertones of cinnamon and violets.

**Syrah:** (see-RAW) A medium bodied wine, with a fruity balance, often with flavors of berries, mocha peppers and other spices.

**Zinfandel:** (ZIN-fan-dell) A strong wine often with a coarse mouth feel and an acidic balance. Flavors may include pepper, blackberries, smoke, nuts and spices.

# Popular BLENDED wines

Blended wines are created from several types of wine grapes. This process allows the wine maker to create an endless array of unique flavors and textures. Table wines are blends. It is necessary that all the grapes used in a blended wine be grown in the same year for a vintage (the year the wine was created) to be on the label.

*Champagne:* (sham-pain) Champagnes   are often a blend of Chardonnay, Pinot Noir and Pinot Meunier grapes.

*Meritage:* (mer-a-tig) A "Meritage" is a New World blended wine created in the Old World style of  Bourdeaux wines (a French blend). A red Meritage most commonly includes a blend of Cabernet Sauvignon, Cabernet Franc, Malbec, Merlot and Petit Verdot grapes. A white Meritage includes a blend of Sauvignon Blanc, Semillón and Sauvignon Vert grapes. The wine maker's goal is to create superior complex wines by enhancing the positive characteristics of the grapes while balancing out the negative characteristics.

*Port:* A powerful, sweet, dessert or after dinner wine with an oily mouth feel. Ports are a blend of several types of grapes fortified with Brandy. The high alcohol content is often balanced with flavors of toast, baked fruit, pepper and black currents.

# WINE TASTING ADVENTURES

ANNETTE DION

# Avila Beach, California
## Day One

Avila Beach is a charming beach town nestled between rolling hills on the central coast of California. I was visiting for a few days with my husband Bob and was pleasantly surprised to find a plethora of small wineries I could visit. My husband is not the wine enthusiast that I am; his enthusiasm is for cars. During our visit my husband would be hunting for car adventures and I would be flying solo on my wine adventures.

We were staying at the San Luis Bay Inn which sits on a hill above Avila Beach and has beautiful views of the ocean and Avila town. The location is great. You can walk to town where they have kayaking and other water sports. I took an early morning walk and scoped out three tasting rooms in the village. Tasting rooms within walking distance from the resort, what more could I ask for? Wait, the Inn will also arrange for a complementary limo to take you tasting. Quick, pinch me. On second thought wait until I have tasted some wine. So many choices. What is a girl to do? I had the Inn sign me up for a limo tasting on Saturday with some other guests. They also handed me coupons for free wine tasting in Avila town. I wasn't staying at this beautiful resort, where I could have coffee while I watched the surf from my private balcony, just for fun. I was here to do research for my book.

It was time to get to work. With coupons in hand I started on my short walk to Avila town. It was Friday evening and the weekly farmers market was in full swing. I could hear the band playing "Mustang Sally" as I headed towards town. It was a beautiful evening. The sun bathed everything and everybody in a golden glow. The ocean sparkled like a pirate's chest of jewels. Gentle breezes played with my long brown hair as I headed out for another wine tasting adventure.

I made my way through the meandering crowd and occasionally stopped to listen to a fiddler playing an Irish jig or to sample home made pie or other treats from the local vendors. I chose to taste the wine maker's wares at Alapay Cellar on First Street. The tasting room is located one block off the main street. When you enter the tasting room you walk through a gift shop that is filled with wine related items on your way to the tasting bar. I made my way to the only empty seat at the tasting bar. Holly, a cheerful server started my tasting by pouring me a Vionginier. I found the Vionginier to be full of flavor, dry and refreshing with undertones of citrus and apricots. I was pleased with the start to this tasting. Debbi Vienna, a vivacious blond with long curly locks, took over the pouring. Debbi had a way of making everyone at the tasting bar feel at ease. With every cork popped we would all shout some type of "cheer" often in a foreign language. I was flying solo for this tasting, yet felt like I was part of the group. To my right was a friendly, newly engaged couple that was only 20 days away from tying the knot. Ahhh, to be in love. To their right was a couple that had been married for years and were members of the wine club. To my left was a group of young women just out of college experiencing their first wine tasting— the virgin wine tasters. To their left was a man visiting from Switzerland. I was in the middle and having a great time.

The next wine poured was a Chardonnay. I am not much of a Chardonnay lover and can usually take them or leave them. I felt the same way about this one. Debbi decided she was going to teach the virgin wine tasters how to blow wine. She had a secret technique (she gave me permission to share it with you) which she learned in her wine travels. I have to admit I have never seen anyone blow wine before. Blowing Wine? Get your mind out of the gutter. Debbi's technique of blowing wine is used to enhance the sniff step when tasting wine. Instead of swirl and sniff you blow and sniff. To do this you hold your glass up near your mouth and blow a quick puff of air into your glass, and for a brief second move the glass away from your mouth allowing the current vapors in the glass to dissipate. Then sniff. It may take a few sniffs before you start to smell the vapors of the wine again. This is a way of isolating and enhancing the bouquet that comes from the wine. It did not take long before Debbi had everyone in the tasting room blowing wine. By the end of our tasting we were all experts, even the virgin wine tasters were blowing wine like pros. As for Debbi, she gets a double gold medal for her blowing talent.

We were now on to the yummy reds. Starting with a 2009 Cabernet Sauvignon. The Cab had a bouquet of cherries, berries and plums. It was spicy with peppery undertones and a long finish. This was followed by a complex Zinfandel with a Jammy finish. Um Um Um.

Next we tasted a Lagrein. Yes, a Lagrein. This was a first for me. A Lagrein is an Italian wine. In the United States this luscious fruit is only harvested by the French Camp vineyards in Paso Robles, California. The wine was dark purple and inky. The flavors are illusive yet spicy and smooth. A double gold winner here. The next pour was Alapays blend, the Altar's. This blend is a combination of Cabernet Franc, Malbec and Lagrein. What a wonderful complex combination. A full bodied red with many subtle undertones of spices, berries and vanilla. This wine would go with anything barbequed or would be great naked.

Next we tasted the Reserve Syrah. The color was beautiful and the flavors balanced. This was followed by the 2008 Rebekah which is named after the wine maker's wife. Every other year for the couple's anniversary the wine maker makes a wine for his lovely wife Rebekah. If Rebekah likes the wine she signs the bottles in gold, with her name, and other little doodles. The bottle we tasted was signed and had a big gold heart on it. If the quality of wine is any indication of the wine maker's love for Rebekah, he must love her very much.

The color of the Rebekah was a deep ruby, the fragrance soft and gentle. The flavor was of rich dark fruit laced with a very subtle sweetness and a finish that lingered. This wine was one to savor. For the grand finale we sampled the 2009 Mosquito. Damn auto spell check. Make that, the 2009 Moscato. This dessert wine had sweet flavors of freshly picked fruits. Perfect for summer parties. Debbi chose to do something I thought I only did. Mix wine. When I had finished about half of my Moscato pour, Debbi added some of the reserve Syrah to my glass. She did this so I could have a party in my mouth, or so she said. It worked. I had a party going on in my mouth. What a fun and intriguing combination of wine. Wine tasting at Alapay was delightful. I learned how to blow wine and experienced some wines that were new to me. I will be sure to stop by next time I visit Avila Beach. I said my good byes to my new tasting buddies, Debbi and Holly. I purchased some wine and headed back out to the farmers market.

   The coastal breeze now had a slight chill as the sun was getting ready to set. I however was feeling warm and cozy. I picked up some fruit and pastries from the vendors and strolled back to the resort. Research can be tough, but someone has to do it.

# Avila Beach, California
## Day Two

I had planned to take the wine tasting limo from the Inn today while my husband went auto crossing. Unfortunately the wine tasting trip was canceled. Now without transportation other than my own two legs I once again set out to Avila town. I still had unused tickets for tastings that I could not let go to waste. As I walked to town the gentle ocean breeze took away my disappointment of missing out on the limo trip. The beach was full of people and Kids were laughing as they played tag with the ocean. Teenagers were having a competitive game of volleyball. The bright sun was shining down on me this warm June afternoon. I had half a notion to just sit on the beach and watch the waves and people at play. Then I remembered I was here to do research and headed to one of the tasting rooms.

I had a few hours before my husband returned from the auto cross track so there was time to taste. I looked at my coupons and chose to taste at Morovino's tasting room. The tasting room is located on a little alcove lined with a variety of shops. The tasting room was small and tastefully decorated with wine related art created by a local artist. I found a seat at the end of the tasting bar and was quickly joined by a young couple from Orange County. They were also staying at the Avila Inn. Damian, our server explained a bit about each of the wines we tasted. He told me that I could use the bar code next to each of the wines, on the flight menu, to access more information using my i-phone. High Tech or what? We tasted a couple Pinot Grigios, a Cabernet and a few blends. My favorite by far was the II Tresoro (The Treasure). It was a velvety dessert wine that had the aromas and flavors of chocolate mixed with raspberries. I thought I had died and gone to heaven. The wine was incredible. I left with two bottles and a smile on my face.

On the other side of the alcove was a new tasting room, 2nd Chance Winery. They were offering free tastings. They only had two wines to taste and I still had time before I would meet up with my husband. No one needed to twist my arm to taste this winery's wares. The young couple I was tasting with at Morovinos tagged along. The tasting room was small and sparsely decorated with artwork done by the wine maker's talented son. Randy, our server was a car guy like my husband. Being a bit of a car girl I had some stories of my own to tell. The four of us had a fun time trading car stories. Randy also liked to cook and shared some recipes using wine that I can hardly wait to try. We tasted a Chardonnay which I enjoyed (remember I am not a Chardonnay lover). We also tasted a Pinot Noir. The Pinot started out with a harsh mouth feel which quickly softened into a nice flavorful wine. Randy said it was a "March wine," it starts out like a Lion and finishes like a Lamb. His words could not have been more true. My tasting time was up and it was time to head back to the resort for the day. My husband had returned and told me that a Porsche with a Chevy engine had been the overall winner at the auto cross. The II Tesoro was the overall winner in my tasting book today.

# SOQUEL MEMORIES

# Soquel, California
## Day One

On this tasting day I chose to taste wine at Bargetto Winery, pronounced BAR-JET-TOE, not Bar-getto. The winery and tasting room is almost hidden within a residential neighborhood. Look closely for the parking lot if you are driving, otherwise you may pass it by. Bargetto Winery has been producing wines in the Santa Cruz mountains since 1933. The Bargetto family emigrated from Piedmont, Italy and established their winery in Soquel, California. Many of the vines used for growing their grapes came from Italy. The Bargetto Winery has become a local icon. I would encourage you to visit one of their tasting rooms, located either on Monterey's Cannery Row, or the one in Soquel which I am visiting on this day trip. Visit, taste and you will understand why Bargetto wines have won so many awards.

Today my mom accompanied me wine tasting. We once lived down the street from Bargetto Winery so I was sure my mom would enjoy a visit to the tasting room. When I was very young, I rode the bus to and from school with some of the Bargetto children who were a little older than I was. The bus would pick them up and drop them off in front of the winery. I cannot say I really knew the children, however when I sat next to Peter on the school bus a few times I remember him to be polite and kind. I understand that Peter has his own winery, Soquel Vineyards, not far from the original Bargetto Winery. I will will write about my trip to his winery later in this book.

This was an especially beautiful February day. The sun was shining warmly when we arrived at Bargetto Winery. The parking lot was full. As I drove in another car pulled out of a parking spot. I recently bought a small SUV. According to the salesman it had been previously owned by a local priest. About as close to being previously owned by a little old lady, wouldn't you say? Oddly enough, since then I find that parking spots seem to open up for me (like the parting of the red sea) and the radio migrates to all the Christian stations without being pre-programmed in. Go figure. Again I digress. Now back to tasting wine.

The gift shop and tasting room were inviting, with the warmth of wood all around. Artwork from previous wine labels hung on the walls and neat displays filled the gift shop. We found the tasting room packed so we decided to browse the gift shop until room at the tasting counter opened up. In the gift shop we found books on wine, beautiful stained glass vases with pictures of grapes and other wine related items. It did not take long for the tasting room to thin as tasters migrated out to the adjoining deck to enjoy the gorgeous day.

My mom and I found our spot at the wine tasting counter and looked at the flight menu for our tasting options. While we were deciding on our tasting flights, our server, Skip (AKA Mr. Wonderful) poured us each a taste of a Brut Sparkling wine which I found balanced, refreshing and a very pleasant start to our tasting. Skip brought us a cookie to clear our palette. We chose to share a reserve and a non reserve tasting (it is perfectly acceptable to split a tasting). Some tasting rooms will do small pours in two separate glasses and others pour the tasting in one glass which you share. Bargetto's is a one glass share tasting room.

We started with a Sauvignon Blanc, which I found to be smooth, light and refreshing. My mom thought it to be light and earthy. Next we tasted Chardonnays, one from the reserve flight and the other from the non reserve flight. The reserve had a fuller body, yet I preferred the complexity of the non reserve. Skip added in a taste of the Vionginier that was not included on the flight menu. Both my mom and I found it to be bright and complex with hints of citrus and lichee. The bouquet and flavors seemed to mirror the beautiful day. There were crackers at the bar for clearing our palette. We then moved on to the reds. I found all the Reds to be superior wines. Many had undertones of cherry, red berries and cedar. The Merlot reminded me of my Dad's best wine, the last batch he made before he passed away. Skip gave us chocolate to eat with our red wines. On the non reserve flight we tried the Black Muscat, a dessert wine, and the port. I enjoyed the Black Muscat. I would prefer to have this wine in place of dessert. It was light and not excessively sweet as I have found many dessert wines to be. The port was very smooth but a little too sweet for my taste. Over all, the tasting was very enjoyable.

There wasn't a single wine that I did not like. Skip was a gracious host and the tasting room was comfortable and unpretentious. I left with a club membership and two bottles of wine, the Black Muscat for me and the Vionginier for my mom.

Feeling relaxed from the tastings and warm from the sunshine we decided to visit some antique shops in Soquel. The village of Soquel is charming in a way that suggests Norman Rockwell may have had something to do with its design. There is a small white church with a tall steeple at one end of town. Then there are several antique shops along Soquel drive, starting just before you reach the town and ending just after you leave the town. It was late in the afternoon and I knew we only had time for a few shops so naturally I decided to start with the shop that I knew would have some wonderful fine art, "Edward and Sons Antiques." Edward was in the shop. I don't think I have ever been in the shop when Edward has not been there. Edward is an entertaining fellow who is willing to share the secrets of Bob Hope's and George Burns' longevity, and the key to success in life. He has stories about his visits with the Rothschilds and what's going on at Christy's auction house. Allow ample time when visiting his shop because once you get Edward started talking you won't want him to stop. It was after 5:00 pm when we said our good byes.

There was no time left for visiting more antique shops. It was time to think about dinner. We were hungry but not famished. After all, we had eaten cookies, crackers and chocolate while tasting wine at Bargetto's. There is a restaurant popular for its old world charm and beautiful gardens with both tourists and locals. This restaurant is known as the Shadowbrook. It is located a short drive from Soquel, above the village of Capitola on Wharf Road. You can choose to walk through the lovely hillside gardens or take a cable car elevator to the restaurant's main entrance. If you are in the area you will not want to miss dining at this restaurant. For a full dinner I suggest you make reservations. The locals know that there is usually room at one of the tables in the bar or at the chef's counter where reservations are not required. The bar menu isn't as extensive as the dining room menu, but there are still many choices.

We sat at the chef's counter and were entertained by Daniel, a young chef who artfully prepared salads and entrées at the speed of light. If someone thought men were not good at multitasking they have never seen Daniel at work. Daniel is a multitasker extraordinaire. We had been sharing wine all day so why not keep the sharing going? Our kindergarten teachers would be so proud. After starting with a glass of wine we ordered a plate of baked brie with jalapeño jelly and crostini. After having tasted wine at Bargetto's earlier in the day I have to admit I was a bit disappointed with the wine I ordered. It just wasn't as good as a Bargetto. I had been in the mood for a red and unfortunately Shadowbrook did not have any Bargetto Cabs or Merlots on the menu. The brie was delicious. Next we ordered the pizza of the day. A flat crust made in a brick oven with imported pepperoni, marinated artichoke hearts, fresh tomatoes, basil and mozzarella. The pizza was just right and it was fun watching Daniel make it. For dessert we split a Jack Daniel's Mud Pie, a necessity when visiting the Shadowbrook Restaurant. By the end of the dinner my mom wanted to hire Daniel for her personal chef. I could not have asked for a better way to spend this beautiful sunny day in February.

# HUNTER HILL

# Soquel, California
## Day Two

My mom and I set out one sunny June afternoon to find Peter Bargetto's tasting room at Soquel Vineyards. The directions we received from a friend were to drive up Glen Haven Road and we would eventually end up at the winery. I didn't bother to look up the address before we left. We drove through beautiful foothills at the base of the Santa Cruz mountains just outside the village of Soquel. We drove for quite a while on the winding road. Each curve in the road would reveal another beautiful scene—a wisteria in bloom, a grove of majestic redwoods or a peaceful meadow full of wild flowers. I was enjoying the drive but after a long while my mom was getting a bit impatient and wanted to turn around and go back to the village to get a bite to eat. "We can have a glass of wine at a restaurant," she pointed out.

I was determined to find Peter's place. Although the beauty of the drive was enchanting, I too started to think that my mom's suggestion to stop at a restaurant may be a good one. Just about the time I was ready to give up on my quest and head back to town we stumbled upon Hunter Hill Vineyard and Winery. We agreed to end our journey at Hunter Hill and see what they had to offer. I will have to hunt down Peter and his winery another time.

In the parking lot we found two tour vans. Considering the drive, we did not expect to find the place buzzing with a wonderful group of university students. There was hardly a place to stand room inside the tasting room. The students were not united by a common major of study or by a college but by a scholarship fund. The students' majors varied from art and literature to science, business and computer technology. At least once a year the students would get together to create and maintain bonds of friendship. Kudos to the ingenuity of the scholarship fund. I had a wonderful conversation with a student who was doing research on how an individual's biological makeup affects the way their body reacts to medications. Medications are not one size fits all. Being a critical care nurse myself this further confirmed what I witnessed in the field of medicine. Medicine is a practice and everyone reacts differently to treatment. Just as each individual has a different preference and responds differently to the aromas and tastes of wine they also react differently to medicine. With some patients you have to give enough sedation to kill an elephant to get them to yawn; and other patients a pinch of benadryl will make them sleep for a whole day. You have to be careful as you never know how someone is going to react. The value of alert clinicians— but I digress.

The winery has a beautifully landscaped area outdoor for tasting as well as an inviting tasting room. Hunter Hill had only one white wine to taste that day, a Sauvignon Blanc. The wine was delicate yet bursting with crisp fruit flavors. Sunshine in a wine glass. My mom found a wine she liked on her first taste and chose to sit in the sun near their waterfall and enjoy a glass, rather than taste a flight. I chose to taste the flight.

The flight included picking six wines off their menu to taste. The menu included mostly red wines. I must say that Van Slatter, Hunter Hill's wine maker, knows what he is doing when it comes to red wines. I enjoyed every one I tasted, which included:

Rock N Rhone blend—A great everyday table red that would go with most foods.

Estate Merlot—Spicy, smoky and full of rich fruit.

Old Vine Zin—Complex, rich, full of body with a jammy finish to savor.

Cabernet Sauvignon—A complex wine with a symphony of spicy fruit flavors and numerous undertones which include chocolate.

Cabernet Franc—Everything that you would expect if you are a Franc lover and more.

Hunter Hill is a family business and the wine maker's lovely wife Christine was pouring wine the day we visited. Christine could not have been a more gracious host and made us feel welcome with her infectious smile. She was very proud of the winery which she and her husband created. This is not the first successful business the couple has created. They are also the foundation for Slatter Construction, another well respected local family business. The couple's focus is now on something they both love—wine.

The entrance to the winery greets visitors with beautiful sunflowers. The outdoor tasting area begins where the rows of grapevines ends. Their lovely rock waterfall is a central focus in the middle of a well manicured lawn. They have shaded picnic tables set out to sit at and enjoy the serene setting. Christine said they welcome people to bring picnic lunches to enjoy while they taste wine. The winery can also order lunches to be delivered for parties. My Mom started working on a guest list for an afternoon lunch at the winery with her girlfriends while she enjoyed her wine. "I know they would all love it up here, it's so lovely," she said with a sigh. That it was. The gurgling of the waterfall and the warm sunshine along with some wonderful wine seemed to make time stop; and for a moment the stress of a busy life melted away. Ahhh....

Hunter Hill was a great find. Just goes to show you, when you are on a quest it is just as important to enjoy the journey as it is to actually get there. I will find Peter Bargetto and his Soquel Vineyards on another adventure. Knowing that I could return to the magical Hunter Hill winery any Saturday or Sunday from 11 am to 4 pm made it easier to leave. I did have a hard time picking out which wines I wanted to take with me. I wanted a bottle of each. I restrained myself and left with only four bottles of wine knowing I would return soon. We said goodbye to our gracious host, Christine, and headed off for a dinner in town.

# SOQUEL VINEYARDS

# Soquel, California
## Day Three

My daughter, Kristina, was home for a short visit and she couldn't have picked a more grey weekend. Mother Nature had extended the foggy, Moss Landing June gloom this year. It was almost the end of August.

We started the day by taking a chilly, dream like walk on a foggy beach near our home. Fishermen and children building sand castles came in and out of view in the mist. As we walked along we made plans for the day. We both were in the mood for sunshine and Peter Bargetto's Soquel Vineyards was still on my list of wineries to visit. We were betting (hoping) that the winery would be located above the fog. We checked out their website (see Appendix C) to find their address and tasting room hours and headed off on another wine tasting adventure.

Once again I found myself driving on scenic Glen Haven Road. The sun was out, Ye ha. Kristina would pause during our conversations to comment on the beauty of the area. Only a few curves in the road past Hunter Hill Winery we found Soquel Vineyards. Soquel Vineyards is nestled in the Santa Cruz mountains above the village of Soquel (and the fog). The views from the vineyard are spectacular, you can see all the way out to the ocean. Well, on a day that the ocean is not fogged in. Today we could see all the way out to the fog. The view was breathtaking nonetheless.

The charming tasting room's roof is made from tiles imported from a winery in Italy that was built in the year 1751. The roof seemed to symbolize roots to the "Old World" of wine making that were deeper than the roots of grape vines. Mary was at the tasting bar and greeted us with a big smile. She informed us we had the option of tasting wine in the tasting room or tasting reserve wines under a gazebo outside. We chose the reserve tasting accompanied by sunshine and the gorgeous view. Al was pouring. Al was very knowledgeable about wine, wine making and growing grapes. I overheard Al giving a short lesson to a couple about bees pollinating the grapes. Wow, a winery where you can have a lesson on the birds and the bees without blushing. Where else can you find that?

Some beautiful Italian music was playing as we tasted wine. A steady steam of wine tasters were having their tastings poured and then walking around the grounds. Some of the tasters chose to sit and enjoy their wine on the lush green lawn between the tasting room and the gazebo. There were girls in excessively short sundresses, thin nerdy looking guys wearing thick rimmed glasses. There were Santa Cruz surfers in shorts and sandals and couples from the Bay area on week end getaways. We sat near the gazebo. A couple whose son was going to be married in a castle in New York next month sat next to us. It was fun listening to them describe the upcoming fairy tale wedding. When they left some of the original "dot-com-ers" sat down. While discussing wine they mentioned they could always pick out Soquel wines by their flavors.

Sunshine, a spectacular view, good music, good wine, good company and interesting characters to watch. What fun. The only thing missing was Peter Bargetto. Al said Peter had bottled wine yesterday and took his family to Monterey for a break. Oh well, his loss.

We tasted some wonderful Pinots made from grapes grown in the Santa Cruz mountains and in Corrolitos, an area about 15 miles south of Soquel. We also tasted a Pinot from grapes grown in the Paso Robles area. My daughter, Kristina, said that the Paso Robles Pinot reminded her of wine she drank when she was in college. She had graduated from Cal Poly San Luis Obispo, which is not far from Paso Robles. The United States uses the "New World" system for naming wine. However you can still recognize a wine's appalachia (area of a origin) by its flavor. Even in the United States. We finished with a Cabernet Franc which was full of flavor and had a long finish that left your mouth feeling a bit fuzzy.

After a good dose of sunshine we headed for the coolness of the tasting room. I wanted to purchase some wine. Olivia was at the tasting bar helping customers and told us we could go around the corner and see where all the barrels are kept, and that Mary was in the barrel room and she could help us with our purchase.

In the barrel room is where I met Paul, Peter's twin brother. I knew by the vineyard's website that Peter had a twin brother but I did not remember him riding the school bus with me as a child. Paul and I spoke for a while and I asked him about the school bus picking up Peter in front of Bargetto Winery. I apologized that I did not remember him. He explained that after kindergarten he went to parochial school and Peter stayed in public school. That explained why I never met Paul. Paul was gregarious, funny and just as nice as I remember his brother to be. Paul made jokes about Peter trying to pick me up on the bus. Yeah right. I rode the bus during my kindergarten through second grade years. During that time I always seemed to have some of my front teeth missing. Such a lovely sight.

I purchased my wine, had a mini photo op with Paul and headed back down the windy road toward Soquel. I wondered why the twins went to different schools after kindergarten. Was it because having identical twins in the same school was too confusing for the teachers or was it some kind of weird family experiment to see how different environments affected the twins? You know they are from a family of wine makers and environments do play a big part in influencing the quality of grapes. How much would different school systems affect the twins? A question to ponder. I should have asked Paul why they went to different schools! The mystery will have to be solved in my next book.

# Appendix A
## References and suggested reading

I have been reading about wine for years and have written this book from the knowledge I've gleaned. Much of the information is general knowledge about wine tasting. I have included references for wine books that are sitting on my book shelf where much of my knowledge about wine tasting was obtained. I have also included websites where I obtained additional information on descriptors. There are no direct quotes in this book. However, since much of the information is common to wine tasting it may appear to be similar in other books.

MacNeil, Karen. **The Wine Bible.** New York: Workman Publishing, 2001.

Narlock, Lori Lyn & Garfinkel, Nancy. **The Wine Lover's Guide to the Wine Country: The Best of Napa, Sonoma, and Mendocino.** San Francisco, California: Cronicle Books, 2005.

Robinson, Jancis. **How to Taste: A Guide to Enjoying Wine.** New York: Simon & Schuster, 2008.

Thomas, Tara Q. **The Complete Idiot's Guide to Wine Basics,** 2nd Edition. New York, New York: Penguin Group, 2008.

**basic-wine-knowledge.com**/wine-definitions.html (2011)

**wine-tastings-guide.com**/wine-descriptions.html (2011)

**world-food-and-wine.com**/describing-wine (2011)

# Appendix B
## Websites

These are the websites for the wineries I visited while doing my research. I would like to thank the gracious hosts at these wineries, who were wonderful teachers.

| | | |
|---|---|---|
| alapaycellars.com | artesawinery.com | bargetto.com |
| boekenoogenwines.com | boetewinery.com | chateaujulien.com |
| chateausinnet.com | elizabethspencerwines.com | folieadeux.com |
| freemarkabbey.com | hellerestate.com | hunterhillwines.com |
| jessupcellers.com | merryvale.com | morovino.com |
| mummnapa.com | pelicanranch.com | pragerport.com |
| reynoldsfamilywinery.com | robertmondavi.com | rochewinery.com |
| rombauervinyards.com | roudonsmith.com | rutherfordgrove.com |
| rutherfordhill.com | sequoiagrove.com | soquelvineyards.com |
| trincheronapavalley.com | stclement.com | stsupery.com |
| turnbullwines.com | ventanawines.com | vsattui.com |

# Appendix C
## Wine Tasting form

Date _____

Comments on Time and Place of Tasting _____

_____

Wine maker_____ Vintage _____

Region _____

Type or Name of Wine _____

Price _____

See: Color & Clarity_____

Swirl: Legs/Tears _____

Sniff: Aroma or Bouquet_____

Sip: Texture & Body _____

Swish or Gargle _____

Swallow or Spit: Finish _____

Rate on a scale of 0-10 (0 = awful and 10 = awesome)_____

# An invitation to you

Now that you know how to taste wine, I would like to invite you to get adventurous, go out wine tasting, then submit your tasting adventures for inclusion in my next book. Only the most interesting and amusing adventures will be chosen.

In exchange for using your adventure you will receive a copy of my next book. In the book you will also be credited as the author of the adventure.

I am doing this because there are way too many wineries and wine tasting rooms for me to visit. I love wine tasting and doing research, however there are more wineries than I could possibly visit in my lifetime. Currently the Napa Valley in California, alone, has over 700 wineries. Napa represents only a small wine region in the world. The sky is the limit when it comes to wine tasting adventures.

If you are interested in submitting your adventures or have questions and comments, please email me at VibrantArt@me.com.


Artfully yours, *Annette*

Artwork
shown in this book
is available for purchase at

# WineTastingArt.com

or

*Vibrant Art Publishing*
831-239-0534 (phone)
831-724-5493 (fax)